✓ W9-BAH-644

BY THE
PEOPLE

E PLURIBUS UNUM

THE U.S. SENATE

Bill McAuliffe

Creative Education ★ Creative Paperbacks

TABLE OF CONTENTS

★ ★ ★

EDMUND G. ROSS Voted against Johnson's dismissal

HIRAM REVELS First black Senate member ▶

ROBERT LA FOLLETTE Challenger of government corruption

HUEY LONG Advocate of government welfare programs

HATTIE CARAWAY First elected female Senate member ▶

ROBERT TAFT Opposer of U.S. involvement in WWII

ROBERT BYRD Longest-serving congressman

HILLARY CLINTON First female senator from New York ▶

Legend has it that Daniel Webster of Massachusetts once won an argument in court with the devil.

THE U.S. SENATE

So when he rose to address the Senate on March 7, 1850, everyone expected a stirring condemnation of slavery, the nation's most divisive issue. But Webster took a surprising approach. "It is fortunate that there is a Senate of the United States," he said. He went on, describing the Senate as "a body to which the country looks with confidence for wise, moderate, patriotic, and healing counsels." Webster offered a compromise historians say held the nation together for another decade. However, he was criticized so intensely that he resigned. A century later, another senator, John F. Kennedy, wrote that Webster's speech was "his greatest act of courageous principle." Indeed, it was one of many instances in which huge personalities have collided with principles in the U.S. Senate, a place where history has been made by the people.

"The Great Compromiser" Henry Clay presented the Compromise of 1850 to the Senate.

SENATE POWERS

ACCEPT  OR REJECT THE PRESIDENT'S NOMINATIONS FOR POSITIONS SUCH AS CABINET OFFICERS, SUPREME COURT JUSTICES, AND AMBASSADORS

HOLD TRIALS FOR GOVERNMENT OFFICIALS WHO HAVE DONE SOMETHING ILLEGAL OR UNETHICAL

APPROVE OR DISAPPROVE TREATIES THE PRESIDENT MAKES

CHAPTER 1

THE UPPER HOUSE

THE U.S. SENATE

The U.S. Senate is often called the greatest **deliberative** body in the world. But it certainly wasn't the first of its kind. The Roman Senate guided rulers of the Roman Empire and the city of Rome for more than 1,000 years, from about 700 B.C. to about A.D. 600. Although some of the Roman Senate's members were elected, there are few similarities to the U.S. Senate other than the name.

The word "senate" comes from the Latin *senex*, meaning "old man." The Roman Senate was, of course, all male. And until 1922, that was also true of the U.S. Senate. But by 2015, 20 percent of American senators were women. The U.S. Senate differs from its ancestor in some other key ways. Its members are now elected directly by the people. And it has the power to stop actions by the executive—that is, the president.

★ **The writers of the Constitution wrestled with the idea of who should make the laws. They wanted to avoid giving that power to one person, such as a king.** ★

THE UPPER HOUSE

Unlike the Roman Senate, the U.S. Senate has a lawmaking counterpart: the House of Representatives. Together, they make up the U.S. Congress. The writers of the Constitution wrestled with the idea of who should make the laws. They wanted to avoid giving that power to one person, such as a king. That's the system they had rebelled against in the Revolutionary War to win independence from Great Britain. As the founders struggled with practical questions, some considered setting up a lawmaking body with representation based on states' populations. Others favored having an equal number of representatives from each state. That way, the most populous states wouldn't make all the policies.

Two Connecticut delegates involved in writing the Constitution, Roger Sherman and Oliver Ellsworth, suggested doing both. So through what became known as the Great Compromise, the Constitution established a **bicameral** legislative body. In the House of Representatives, the number of delegates would be based on population. In the Senate, two delegates would represent each state. Today, there are 435 members of the House of Representatives from the 50 states. California alone has 53. But the Senate has only 100 members. California has two senators, as does every other state, no matter its population.

According to historian Moncure D. Conway, in 1789, Thomas Jefferson asked

EDMUND G. ROSS OF KANSAS IS REMEMBERED FOR CASTING ONE OF THE MOST CRITICAL VOTES IN THE NATION'S HISTORY. STRONGLY OPPOSED TO SLAVERY, ROSS WAS ELECTED IN 1866. HE WAS EXPECTED TO JOIN FELLOW REPUBLICANS IN VOTING FOR THE IMPEACHMENT OF PRESIDENT ANDREW JOHNSON. MANY REPUBLICANS FROM THE NORTH THOUGHT JOHNSON SHOULD HAVE TREATED SOUTHERN STATES MORE HARSHLY AFTER THE CIVIL WAR. BUT ROSS VOTED AGAINST THE MEASURE, WHICH FAILED BY ONE VOTE. ROSS LATER SAID HE VOTED TO PROTECT THE GOVERNMENT'S SEPARATION OF POWERS FROM THE DANGEROUS "SWAY OF GREAT MAJORITIES." REPUBLICANS BRANDED HIM A TRAITOR, AND HE SERVED ONLY ONE TERM.

WE THE PEOPLE

★ EDMUND G. ROSS ★

George Washington why the new constitution had been written to include a second legislative house. Washington responded with a question of his own. "Why did you pour that tea into your saucer?" Washington asked. "To cool it," Jefferson replied. "Even so, we pour our legislation into the senatorial saucer to cool it," Washington said. So the Senate has sometimes been called "the saucer that cools the tea (or coffee)."

To make laws, the House and Senate both create bills and debate them. When the Senate approves a bill, it passes the measure over to the House, which can make changes, and vice versa. If there are enough votes for a bill to pass in each house, it goes to the president, who signs it into law.

But the Senate has some powers the House doesn't. Under the Constitution, the

HIRAM REVELS WAS THE FIRST BLACK SENATOR.

He was elected from Mississippi as the state was readmitted to the Union in 1870. Revels filled the seat that had belonged to Jefferson Davis before Davis became president of the Confederate States of America. Revels was a minister in the African Methodist Episcopal Church. He organized two black regiments for the Union Army during the Civil War. Revels left the Senate after only one year to become president of the newly established Alcorn University. The second black person elected to the Senate was Blanche Bruce, in 1875. Bruce was the last black senator until 1967.

WE THE PEOPLE

★ HIRAM REVELS ★

Senate is able to sign treaties with other nations. It votes on the president's nominations to the Supreme Court and other federal courts, as well as to the cabinet, ambassadorships, and other federal agencies. And if the House votes to remove a president or other high-ranking federal official from office, the Senate conducts a trial on the charges against that person.

Another feature unique to the Senate is its capacity for debate. Some say this is the source of its glory. Others say it has brought the work of the Senate to a grinding halt in recent years. Originally, senators could talk as long as they wanted. In the decades before the Civil War, senators such as Daniel Webster, John C. Calhoun, and Henry Clay emerged as some of the greatest orators in Senate history.

In 1917, the Senate allowed debate to

be cut off if two-thirds of the senators voted to do so. In 1975, that was shaved to three-fifths, or 60 of the Senate's 100 members. Lengthy speeches known as filibusters are often used to block legislation from being voted upon. They show how the Senate gives tremendous power to the minority, and

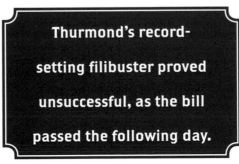

Thurmond's record-setting filibuster proved unsuccessful, as the bill passed the following day.

even to individual voices. In 1957, Strom Thurmond of South Carolina spoke for 24 hours and 18 minutes to prevent a vote on the Civil Rights Act. To prepare, Thurmond reportedly took steam baths to dehydrate himself. During the speech, he went to the bathroom only once, when another senator asked Thurmond for

> ★ Many political observers say that in recent years [the Senate] has lost stature because of bickering among the parties. But in some ways, that's nothing new. ★

a few minutes to speak. Thurmond finally sat down after doctors warned him he was risking kidney damage. Thurmond's marathon ranks as the Senate speaking record.

The Senate is called the "upper" chamber as a historical reference to its first meeting place. When the first Congress gathered at New York City's Federal Hall in 1789, the Senate met upstairs. Long debates and six-year terms—longer than the president's or representatives'—have given the Senate a reputation for careful deliberation. Many political observers say that in recent years it has

Congress met in Philadelphia for 10 years before moving to the U.S. Capitol building in Washington, D.C.

lost stature because of bickering among the parties. But in some ways, that's nothing new. In 1850, the heat rose to an intense level between Henry Foote of Mississippi and Thomas Hart Benton of Missouri. As they debated a proposal that would limit the expansion of slavery, Benton strode toward Foote's desk. Foote, who was known to be extremely short-tempered and had been wounded three times in duels, drew a pistol. Spectators as well as senators bolted from the Senate chamber. "I have no pistols!" Benton reportedly said as he tore open his vest. "Stand out of the way

THE FIRST UNITED STATES CONGRESS, 1789–91

AT FEDERAL HALL
New York City, New York

SESSION 1: March 4, 1789—September 29, 1789
SESSION 2: January 4, 1790—August 12, 1790

PENNSYLVANIA

NEW JERSEY

RHODE ISLAND

WEST TERRITORY

AT CONGRESS HALL
Philadelphia, Pennsylvania

SESSION 3: December 6, 1790—March 3, 1791

SOUTH CAROLINA

The **RESIDENCE ACT OF 1790** made Philadelphia the nation's temporary capital city.

THE UPPER HOUSE

and let the assassin fire!" No shots were fired, though. Someone grabbed the gun from Foote's hand, perhaps saving Benton from injury and allowing Foote to save face, at the very least. Things cooled in the Senate for a time after that. But a half century later, in 1902, one of South Carolina's senators punched the other one on the Senate floor after an argument.

However, hotheadedness and impulsiveness have not been typical of the Senate. Instead, its hallmark has been a respectful spirit of time-consuming compromise. "The Senate is often castigated for its inefficiency, but in fact, it was never intended to be efficient," said Robert Byrd of West Virginia, a noted Senate historian who himself served for 51 years. "Its purpose was and is to examine, consider, protest, and to be a totally independent source of wisdom and judgment on the actions of the lower House and on the executive. As such, the Senate is the central pillar of our Constitutional system."

> Thomas Hart Benton (opposite) supported westward expansion and opposed the spread of slavery into new territories.

SLAVERY

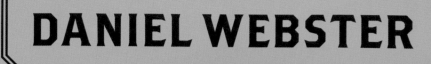

DANIEL WEBSTER

WESTWARD EXPANSION

INTERNATIONAL RELATIONS

ECONOMIC POLICIES

STEPHEN A. DOUGLAS

INDIAN TREATIES

HENRY CLAY

CANAL-BUILDING

INDUSTRIALIZATION

JEFFERSON DAVIS

JOHN C. CALHOUN

CHAPTER 2

SENATE STANDOUTS

THE U.S. SENATE

The period from the late 1830s through the 1850s is often regarded as the "Golden Era" of the U.S. Senate. With the nation divided over slavery, presidents were often compromise candidates, overshadowed and outlasted by senators. There were eight presidents from 1837 to 1861; none served more than a single term, and two died in office.

Meanwhile, in the Senate, some of the great issues of American history were being debated. Slavery. Westward expansion and the addition of new states. **Industrialization**, canal-building, and economic policy. Indian treaties. The young country's international relationships. With the newly invented telegraph communicating news from Washington throughout the expanding nation, senators rose to great heights of fame during that time. Daniel Webster was foremost among them.

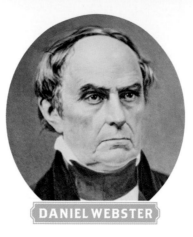

DANIEL WEBSTER

★ Webster became famous for an 1830 speech that redefined the nation.... By 1850, Webster was regarded as a likely presidential candidate. ★

SENATE STANDOUTS

First elected to the Senate in 1827, Webster became famous for an 1830 speech that redefined the nation. The unrehearsed speech about federal land sales is known as the Second Reply to Hayne. It was Webster's response to senator Robert Hayne's assertion that states had the right to resist federal laws they thought exceeded the federal government's authority. Webster thought that would be a recipe for chaos. He argued that the Constitution was the supreme law of the land. The speech changed the U.S. "from a plural to a singular noun," according to the editor of Webster's papers. By 1850, Webster was regarded as a likely presidential candidate. But his support of the Compromise of 1850 cost him the backing of antislavery

groups and others across the North. He resigned from the Senate in 1850 and served as secretary of state until his death in 1852.

The 1850 Compromise began as a way to admit California to the Union as a free state. (Free states did not allow slavery.) Henry Clay of Kentucky introduced several measures to keep a balance between free and slave states. Clay's congressional career spanned either side of the Golden Era: he served from 1806 to 1852 in four separate stretches. In 1820, while in the House of Representatives between senate terms, Clay proposed the Missouri Compromise. This admitted Missouri as a slave state and Maine as a free state. It also set limits on slavery's expansion. In 1834, Clay engineered

ATTORNEY ROBERT LA FOLLETTE OF

WISCONSIN HAD JUST LOST A BID FOR REELEC-
TION TO THE U.S. HOUSE IN 1890 WHEN A STATE
REPUBLICAN LEADER OFFERED HIM A BRIBE TO "FIX"
A COURT CASE HE WAS WORKING ON. OUTRAGED,
LA FOLLETTE SOON BECAME KNOWN AS "FIGHTING
BOB." HE ATTACKED LUMBER AND RAILROAD INTER-
ESTS AND GOVERNMENT CORRUPTION ALIKE. HE WAS
ELECTED TO THE U.S. SENATE IN 1906. HE SUPPORTED
THE LABOR MOVEMENT BUT OPPOSED U.S. INVOLVEMENT
IN WORLD WAR I, FOR WHICH HE WAS BRANDED UNPA-
TRIOTIC. HE WAS REELECTED THREE TIMES AND IN 1924
RAN FOR PRESIDENT ON THE PROGRESSIVE TICKET.

★ ROBERT LA FOLLETTE ★

a Senate **censure** of president Andrew Jackson after a fight over national banking policy. That show of Senate power was the only censure of a president in history. The 1850 Compromise, drawn up by Clay and supported by Webster, was another controversial plan that historians say delayed the Civil War. Clay was an unsuccessful candidate for president four times. But after he died in 1852, his funeral was the first to be held in the Capitol Rotunda.

Other giants also held senate seats in that era. John C. Calhoun of South Carolina served 16 years in the Senate. Before that, he spent eight years as vice president under John Quincy Adams and Andrew Jackson. He was the Senate's most forceful champion of states' rights to resist federal laws they considered unconstitutional. (Such an argument was key to supporting slavery in the 1800s.

GUIDED BY HIS MOTTO "EVERY MAN A KING," LOUISIANA'S HUEY LONG WAS ONE OF THE MOST POPULAR YET DISTRUSTED POLITICAL FIGURES OF THE 1930S. ELECTED GOVERNOR IN 1928 BY THE WIDEST MARGIN IN STATE HISTORY, HE ENTERED THE U.S. SENATE IN 1932. WITH CLEAR PRESIDENTIAL AMBITIONS, HE PROMOTED A PLAN TO SHIFT WEALTH FROM THE RICH AND PROVIDE A GOVERNMENT-SUPPORTED BASIC INCOME FOR THE POOR. FROM WASHINGTON, LONG CONTINUED WHAT SOME SAID WAS DICTATORIAL CONTROL OF STATE GOVERNMENT IN LOUISIANA, WHERE HE WAS KNOWN AS "THE KINGFISH." HE WAS SHOT TO DEATH IN 1935 BY A POLITICAL OPPONENT'S RELATIVE. HE WAS 42.

WE THE PEOPLE

★ HUEY LONG ★

It was later used against civil rights legislation in the mid-1900s.) Jefferson Davis of Mississippi served eight years in the Senate, but after Mississippi's **secession** in 1861, he became president of the Confederate States of America. Stephen A. Douglas of Illinois served three terms in the Senate before his death in 1861. He is best known for the debates he had during the 1858 campaign with a one-term congressman named Abraham Lincoln.

Douglas may have won the Senate seat, but Lincoln won the presidency two years later.

Around that time, some of the daily practicalities of life in the Senate began to change. From 1819 to 1859, the Senate met in a room that seated only 64. But because the country was adding more states, a new chamber was built. The Senate has met there ever since. The so-called Old Senate Chamber is still used for closed hearings or for times when

senators want to be particularly attuned to history. For example, Senate leaders met in the Old Senate Chamber to set rules for the impeachment trial of president Bill Clinton in 1999.

Until a century ago, senators worked mostly at their desks on the Senate floor. They moved into offices in what is now the Russell Senate

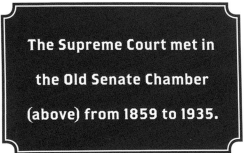

The Supreme Court met in the Old Senate Chamber (above) from 1859 to 1935.

Office Building in 1909. But being a Senator wasn't even a full-time job until 1934, partly because summers in Washington, D.C. were too hot in the days before air conditioning.

Although the Constitution declares that the vice president is the chief presiding officer (or "president") of the Senate, the last vice

ABRAHAM LINCOLN

★ **During the Civil War, Lincoln greatly extended presidential powers. The presidency began to overshadow both the Senate and the House.** ★

SENATE STANDOUTS

president to attend on a regular basis was Alben Barkley. He left office in 1953. The job now rotates among all members of the Senate. The vice president, who can vote only to break a tie, shows up when votes on controversial bills are scheduled.

During the Civil War, Lincoln greatly extended presidential powers. The presidency began to overshadow both the Senate and the House. By the late 1800s, senators had lost power and respect. Because senators at that time were chosen by members of state legislatures, power in the Senate reflected power in those state bodies.

> Lincoln called for volunteer soldiers and funded the Union's wartime efforts without congressional approval.

U.S. senators tended to concentrate more on state and local issues than on national and international affairs. Big donors to political parties were often rewarded with Senate seats; **bribery** and corruption were common.

The first time senators were elected by popular vote was in 1914. The process still differs from state to state, but the role of political parties is central. Each party usually nominates a senatorial candidate. This gives him or her a tremendous amount of visibility and financial support. It also provides a huge network of professional help as well as numerous

SENATE LEADERSHIP

PRESIDENT OF THE SENATE

The U.S. vice president also serves as the president of the Senate; however, the vice president rarely attends Senate meetings and does not cast a vote unless Senate members are equally divided.

PRESIDENT PRO TEMPORE

Traditionally, the president pro tempore is the longest-serving senator of the majority party. The president pro tempore presides over the Senate, enforces Senate rules, and votes on legislation.

MAJORITY AND MINORITY LEADERS

The Senate majority and minority leaders serve as the spokespersons for their respective political parties. The leaders work to unite their parties and keep legislation moving through the Senate.

SENATE OFFICERS AND OFFICIALS

CHAPLAIN

The Senate chaplain opens each meeting with a prayer and provides counseling and spiritual services to Senate members, families, and staff. The chaplain also conducts regular prayer meetings and organizes a weekly breakfast.

PARTY SECRETARIES

Party secretaries schedule legislation for the Senate floor and ensure senators are informed of pending legislation. The secretaries also keep senators updated on roll-call votes, which require every member to cast a vote.

SERGEANT AT ARMS

The sergeant at arms is responsible for safety, security, and order in the Senate chamber. The sergeant may compel absent members to the floor and arrest anyone who violates Senate rules.

SECRETARY OF THE SENATE

The Secretary of the Senate oversees several offices, maintains Senate records, and manages administrative and financial aspects such as asset management, information technology, and payroll.

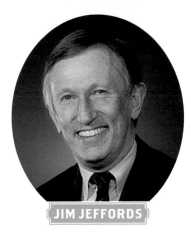

JIM JEFFORDS

SENATE STANDOUTS

campaign volunteers.

Parties remain critical within the Senate itself. Senate leaders, as well as the chairs of the Senate's 20 committees and 68 subcommittees, are chosen by the majority party. The committees determine how bills proceed through the Senate. Even though the Senate has always had an even number of members, membership has been evenly divided by party (without any independent or third-party members) only once in history. That was for six months in 2001, when the Senate was divided exactly 50-50 between Republicans and Democrats. The balance changed when Jim Jeffords of Vermont announced that he was leaving the Republican Party to become an Independent. That gave the Democrats majority status.

Senate majority and minority leaders are elected by their respective political parties at the beginning of each new Congress, or every two years.

THE HOUSE VOTED TO IMPEACH PRESIDENT JOHNSON.

In 1867, as President Johnson's relationship with Congress continued to deteriorate, the legislative branch passed the Tenure of Office Act over the executive's veto. The act required Senate-confirmed officials to remain in office until the Senate had approved a successor. Within months, Johnson defied the act by suspending secretary of war Edwin M. Stanton and replacing him with General Ulysses S. Grant. On Congress's orders, Stanton was reinstated. He was back in office for little more than a month when Johnson fired him. The House impeached Johnson for violating the Tenure of Office Act; the Senate carried out his impeachment trial in the spring of 1868.

THE SENATE CONDUCTED A TRIAL TO DECIDE WHETHER JOHNSON WOULD BE REMOVED FROM OFFICE.

CHAPTER № 3

WORKING THE LEVERS OF POWER

=== **THE U.S. SENATE** ===

The Civil War was the product of tensions that had been building since the nation's founding more than 70 years before. The four-year war ended in 1865, but some very hard feelings remained. One of the places where they emerged was the U.S. Senate.

The year 1868 saw something new happen in Congress. The Civil War had ended only three years before. Lincoln had been assassinated days after the Confederate surrender, and his vice president, Andrew Johnson, had become president. Many congressmen thought Johnson was being too gentle with the former Confederate states as they reentered the Union. Then they argued he had illegally tried to fire the secretary of war. The U.S. House voted to impeach him. The Senate conducted a trial to decide whether Johnson would be removed from office.

★ Impeachment trials are one of the powers given only to the Senate by the Constitution. ★

WORKING THE LEVERS OF POWER

After three weeks of testimony, it was time to vote. If two-thirds of the senators (36) voted against him, Johnson was out. When the roll was called, only 35 senators favored impeachment. Johnson remained in office for the rest of his term, until 1869. In 1875, he was elected to the Senate from Tennessee. He became both the first president to be impeached and the first former president to serve in the Senate.

Historians have noted that the Johnson impeachment vote was more about protecting the presidency from an angry Congress than it was about the particular violations Johnson supposedly committed. And 131 years later, the outcome was even more emphatic when a Republican-controlled Senate declined to convict Democratic president Bill Clinton. Senate minority leader Tom Daschle of South Dakota later wrote that he and majority leader Trent Lott of Mississippi had considered how "the fabric of our nation might be torn beyond repair if the Senate trial degenerated into the same spectacle as the House impeachment."

Impeachment trials are one of the powers given only to the Senate by the Constitution. Another is the power to "advise and consent" to treaties and presidential appointments. In 1789, President Washington and his secretary of war, Henry Knox, asked the Senate to "advise and consent" to a treaty with the Creek Nation. From that point on, the Senate has

★ HATTIE CARAWAY ★

HATTIE CARAWAY OF ARKANSAS WAS THE FIRST WOMAN ELECTED TO THE U.S. SENATE. AFTER HER HUSBAND THADDEUS DIED IN 1931, SHE WAS APPOINTED TO FILL HIS SEAT. SHE WAS ELECTED ON HER OWN IN 1932 AND BECAME THE FIRST WOMAN TO PRESIDE OVER THE SENATE. SHE WAS ALSO THE FIRST WOMAN TO CHAIR A SENATE COMMITTEE, THE ENROLLED BILLS COMMITTEE. CARAWAY WAS ELECTED TO A SECOND TERM IN 1938 AND REMAINED COMMITTEE CHAIR UNTIL 1945. ALTHOUGH THREE OTHER WOMEN SERVED IN THE SENATE IN THE 1930S, ALL WERE APPOINTED. NONE SOUGHT ELECTION ON HER OWN AS CARAWAY HAD.

strongly pursued its right to review treaties and appointments, making the nomination process a key Senate check on presidential power. Today, presidents usually ask for Senate guidance before announcing a nomination, particularly to the Supreme Court.

But nominations can also be where conflicts arise. The president and the Senate may fight over the attitudes and values they want to promote. Federal judges, after all, are appointed for life and can contribute to a president's long-term legacy. Only two presidents, Richard Nixon and Grover Cleveland, had two nominees rejected.

In 1987, president Ronald Reagan nominated federal judge Robert Bork to fill an opening on the Supreme Court. As **solicitor general** in 1973, Bork had become known as the man who had fired the special prosecutor in the **Watergate scandal** investigations at President Nixon's orders. Members of Congress who suspected Bork would favor too much of Reagan's agenda reacted strongly. Ted Kennedy of Massachusetts, in an often-quoted statement, said Reagan and Bork would impose a "reactionary vision of the Constitution on the Supreme Court and the next generation of Americans." Bork was ultimately rejected on a 58–42 vote, one of the widest margins ever. The nominee who followed him, Anthony Kennedy, was approved unanimously in 1988. As of 2016, Justice Kennedy was still casting "swing" votes between conservative and liberal groups.

In 1991, Clarence Thomas was nominated to the Supreme Court by president George H. W. Bush. Thomas was criticized by some civil rights groups for opposing what had been seen as legal gains for

minorities. But those issues got lost when law professor Anita Hill, a former colleague of Thomas's, accused him of sexual harassment. The hearings exploded into a national media event. Nevertheless, Thomas was confirmed 52-48, a narrow margin but a victory for Bush.

The Senate can also wield significant power by conducting investigations. These can venture into any subject, and they sometimes have great historical impact. In 1922, the Senate Committee on Public Lands followed up on a news report claiming that Albert Fall, the secretary of the interior, had leased a naval petroleum reserve to a private oil company.

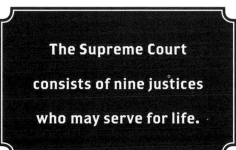

The Supreme Court consists of nine justices who may serve for life.

★ The Teapot Dome scandal stained the brief presidency of Warren G. Harding. ★

WORKING THE LEVERS OF POWER

The Wyoming reserve, an area intended to produce oil for the Navy, was near a rock formation known as Teapot Dome. The Senate investigation found that Fall, a former senator from New Mexico, had accepted bribes to make the lease possible. He became the first cabinet officer to go to prison for crimes committed in office. The Teapot Dome scandal stained the brief presidency of Warren G. Harding.

Fifty years later, the Senate launched another important investigation. This was about a 1972 burglary at the Democratic National Committee headquarters at the Watergate Hotel in Washington, D.C. A captivated nation watched on television as the Senate committee, led by Sam Ervin of North Carolina, ultimately uncovered a web of criminal activities. Some of President Nixon's closest advisers and cabinet officers were found guilty. Nixon himself came under suspicion. The House soon drew up articles of impeachment. But Nixon resigned before a trial could start.

Senate investigations —or the threat of them— have also disgraced the Senate itself. As the **Cold War** intensified in the early 1950s, Wisconsin senator Joseph McCarthy launched a search for **communists** in the State Department. His committee charged thousands of Americans of being suspected spies. Widely publicized hearings were conducted. In the end, McCarthy wasn't able to prove any of his claims. In 1954, after a significant counterattack during an investigation into U.S. Army affairs, the

> Political cartoons incorporated the U.S. Capitol and a teapot to depict the high-level corruption of the Teapot Dome scandal.

DISGRACED SENATORS

WILLIAM BLOUNT

Expelled in 1797 for treason and conspiracy

THOMAS CLINGMAN

One of 14 senators expelled in 1861 for taking up arms against the Union

BENJAMIN R. TILLMAN

Censured in 1902 for fighting on the Senate floor

JOSEPH MCCARTHY

Condemned in 1954 for abuse of power and conduct unbecoming of a senator

JOHN ENSIGN

Charged in 2011 for financial improprieties and ethics violations

Although the Senate has censured many of its members, it has expelled only 15 senators.

WILLIAM SEBASTIAN

WORKING THE LEVERS OF POWER

Senate voted 67–22 to censure McCarthy. "McCarthyism" emerged as a term describing drummed-up scare tactics and unfounded personal attacks.

Although impeachment trials against presidents have happened twice, only once has a senator had a close call. In 1797, the House charged William Blount of Tennessee of working with the British to seize Florida and other parts of the Louisiana Territory. The Senate immediately voted to expel Blount. It began a trial at the end of 1798 but dismissed the charges against him two months later. In the days leading up to the Civil War, 14 senators were expelled for sympathizing with the Confederacy. All were Southern Democrats. Of those, only William Sebastian of Arkansas later had his expulsion overturned.

> No one has been expelled from the Senate since the 14 Confederate supporters were removed from office in 1861.

SENATE MEMBER REQUIREMENTS

BE A RESIDENT OF THE STATE THEY REPRESENT AT THE TIME OF THE ELECTION

HAVE BEEN A CITIZEN OF THE UNITED STATES FOR THE PAST ★ 9 ★ YEARS

BE AT LEAST 30 YEARS OLD

Chapter

CHAPTER NO 4

"EVERYBODY DISAGREES"

THE U.S. SENATE

Throughout the 19th century, people across the U.S. recognized the mounting problems with the way senators were elected. Increasingly, it seemed as though state governments had too much influence at the federal level. There were dozens of attempts to fix this. Six times, the House tried to change the Constitution. But the Senate did not go along until 1912. In 1913, ratification of the 17th Amendment to the Constitution meant that voters would directly elect senators.

In 2015, 13 states had a senator from each of the major parties. Twenty states were represented by Republicans alone. Fifteen had only Democrats. The remaining two states split evenly; one had an Independent and a Republican senator, and the other an Independent and a Democrat. That would seem to reflect how closely American voters are divided. Of course, many say that also explains why Congress, and the Senate in particular, has

37

★ Today, the filibuster ... is a key feature of the government's system of checks and balances. But it has also been seen as a key symptom of "gridlock" in Washington—the failure to agree as a show of power. ★

"EVERYBODY DISAGREES"

struggled in recent years to accomplish even the most basic tasks. But there are other factors as well.

Until 1971, filibusters were relatively rare in the Senate. Fewer than 10 occurred during most congressional sessions. But in the 113th Congress of 2013–15, there were 253. Many filibusters happened over basic orders of business, such as preliminary motions to proceed.

Today, the filibuster gives individual senators the power to prevent a vote, particularly on judicial nominations. It is a key feature of the government's system of checks and balances. But it has also been seen as a key symptom of "gridlock" in Washington—the failure to agree as a show of power. "Intense

partisan polarization has raised the stakes in every debate and on every vote, making it difficult to lose with grace and nearly impossible to compromise without cost," said Christopher Dodd of Connecticut in his 2010 farewell address. "Americans' distrust of politicians provides compelling incentives for senators to distrust each other, to disparage this very institution, and to disengage from the policymaking process."

In 2013, the Senate changed its rules to allow a simple majority—51 members— to end a filibuster on some procedures. (A notable exception was for Supreme Court nominations.) Some political observers felt this would remove some of the protection the Senate has always extended to minority

★ ROBERT BYRD ★

THE SENATE'S LEADING PERSONALITY IN RECENT YEARS MAY HAVE BEEN ROBERT BYRD OF WEST VIRGINIA. BYRD SERVED THREE TERMS IN THE HOUSE OF REPRESENTATIVES BEFORE ENTERING THE SENATE IN 1959. WHILE IN CONGRESS, HE ATTENDED NIGHT SCHOOL TO EARN A LAW DEGREE. IN HIS 51 YEARS IN THE SENATE, BYRD BECAME AN AUTHORITY ON SENATE HISTORY, GIVING TALKS TO FIRST-TERM SENATORS. HE MADE HISTORY AS WELL. HE WAS THE LONGEST-SERVING SENATOR AND, WITH HIS TIME IN THE HOUSE, THE SECOND-LONGEST-SERVING CONGRESSMAN. HE WAS ALSO AN ACCOMPLISHED FIDDLER. BYRD HAD ONCE BEEN A LEADER IN THE KU KLUX KLAN, BUT HE LATER REFUSED TO BE ASSOCIATED WITH THAT GROUP.

members. But others argued that filibusters have become a tool of the minority to stall work. Lowering the number of votes needed to end debate might get more legislation moving again.

Sarah Binder, a professor of political science at George Washington University, takes a different view. The filibuster was never a grand effort on behalf of minority rights, she argues. Instead, it came out of some tinkering with the rulebook in 1806. In fact, Binder says, the House and Senate originally had the same rule that allowed a simple majority to cut off debate. But the Senate allowed the rule to disappear at the vice president's request.

Senators are often quite willing to vote, and they take it seriously. After undergoing emergency surgery in 1985, Pete Wilson of California took an ambulance to the Senate

IN 2015, AS SHE ANNOUNCED HER SECOND BID TO BECOME THE FIRST FEMALE PRESIDENT, HILLARY CLINTON HAD ALREADY ACCOMPLISHED NUMEROUS FIRSTS. AS THE WIFE OF BILL CLINTON, SHE WAS FIRST LADY OF ARKANSAS, THEN FIRST LADY OF THE U.S. IN 2000, SHE WAS THE FIRST WOMAN ELECTED AS A SENATOR FROM NEW YORK. SHE VOTED IN FAVOR OF SOME OF THE EARLY MEASURES SUPPORTING U.S. MILITARY INVOLVEMENT IN AFGHANISTAN AND IRAQ. SHE SERVED IN THE SENATE UNTIL 2009, WHEN PRESIDENT OBAMA, HER CHALLENGER FOR THE DEMOCRATIC PRESIDENTIAL NOMINATION IN 2008, APPOINTED HER SECRETARY OF STATE. SHE HELD THAT POSITION UNTIL 2013.

WE THE PEOPLE

★ HILLARY CLINTON ★

at 2:00 A.M. He didn't want to miss voting on a budget deficit measure. His colleagues gave him a standing ovation. Of course, casting a vote is sometimes the last thing senators want to do, if the issue is controversial enough. In 1987, Senate Republicans, in support of a filibuster preventing a vote on campaign finance reform, scattered throughout the Capitol. Byrd, the Democratic majority leader at the time, ordered the sergeant-at-arms to arrest those who were absent. Bob Packwood of Oregon was carried feet-first into the chamber to cast a reluctant vote.

Although each Senate term is for six years, the terms are staggered. Every two years, a third of the senators are in an election campaign. Many critics consider campaigning a distraction that, in recent years, has become more demanding. The greatest demands are, of course, for money and the

time required to raise it.

In 1968, Vermonter George Aiken spent $17.09 on his reelection campaign. But in 2012, candidates spent an average of $10.4 million to win a Senate seat. This was more than double what they had spent 10 years before. Meanwhile, groups outside the candidates' campaigns spent $457 million on Senate and House races in 2012, compared with $9 million in 1986. Most of that 50-fold increase can be traced to a 2010 Supreme Court decision that lifted limits on how much political action committees could spend on advertising and other "outside" support for candidates.

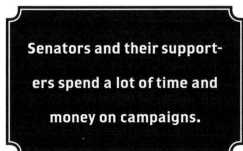

Senators and their supporters spend a lot of time and money on campaigns.

★ **Although nearly 51 percent of the U.S. population was female in 2014, only 20 percent of senators were women. Racial minority representation is even worse.** ★

"EVERYBODY DISAGREES"

One of the Senate's strengths has always been that its members must appeal to a far wider range of voters than do representatives. However, the makeup of the Senate does not reflect the diversity of the population. Although nearly 51 percent of the U.S. population was female in 2014, only 20 percent of senators were women. Racial minority representation is even worse. In 2015, the Senate had only two black members, three Hispanics, one Asian American, and no Native Americans. Arturo Vargas, executive director of the National Association of Latino Elected and Appointed Officials, said he expected more minorities to get elected to Congress in the coming years. But because most officeholders get reelected, and most are white, many will have to retire before that happens.

Former Senate majority leader Tom Daschle liked to repeat the adage that the Senate is "the only place in the country where somebody stands up to speak, nobody listens, and then everybody disagrees." Daschle also wrote that he believes the modern Senate may be plagued by conditions that can't be easily changed. Easier modes of travel give

Hiram Fong, a senator of Hawaii from 1959 to 1977, was the first Asian American to serve in the Senate.

CALIFORNIA
POPULATION IN 2014
38,800,000

EACH SENATOR REPRESENTS
19,400,000 PEOPLE

WYOMING
POPULATION IN 2014
584,150

EACH SENATOR REPRESENTS
292,075 PEOPLE

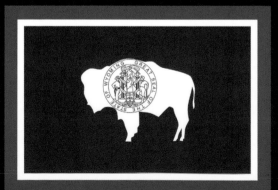

= 250,000 PEOPLE

DANIEL WEBSTER

"EVERYBODY DISAGREES"

senators more flexibility to get back home to meet with **constituents**. But if they are often traveling, their schedule when they are in Washington is intensified. They may not get to know each other in the way senators once did. Historically, such personal connections have helped forge bonds and a sense of mutual respect in the Senate.

Nearly 200 years ago, Daniel Webster had quite a different view of the Senate, which was just beginning to enter one of its most illustrious periods. He called it "a body not yet moved from its propriety, not lost to a just sense of its own dignity and its own high responsibilities."

Clearly, times have changed the Senate. But some things about it are the same as they were when it met for the first time in 1789. Two senators still represent each state. And it remains a work in progress.

> The number of representatives per state adjusts according to each 10-year census, but the number of senators remains the same.

bicameral describing a lawmaking body having two branches or chambers

bribery paying for favors that are illegal or not available to others

censure an official condemnation, a mark of strong disapproval

Cold War the hostile competition between the U.S. and its allies against the Soviet Union and its allies from the end of World War II to the collapse of the Soviet Union in 1991

communists people who advocate giving economic power to workers instead of business owners and were sympathetic to the Soviet Union during the Cold War

constituents the people an elected official represents

deliberative designed to discuss policies and procedures in detail; more involved in thought and analysis than action

impeachment a process of bringing formal charges against a government official for crimes committed while in office

industrialization the introduction of manufacturing and other technical enterprises into a region or economy that had been rural, agricultural, or undeveloped

partisan polarization the separation of political groups based on extreme ideas and attitudes

secession withdrawal from an alliance

solicitor general the official who oversees court cases involving the U.S. that go to the Supreme Court; he or she often personally argues the government's case before the court

vetoed cancelled by an executive after being approved by others

Watergate scandal the events that led to the resignation of president Richard M. Nixon; it began with a burglary at the Watergate Hotel in Washington, D.C.

SELECTED BIBLIOGRAPHY

Daschle, Tom, and Charles Robbins. *The U.S. Senate: Fundamentals of American Government*. New York: Thomas Dunne Books, 2013.

Gould, Lewis L. *The Most Exclusive Club: A History of the Modern United States Senate*. New York: Basic Books, 2005.

Kennedy, John F. *Profiles in Courage*. New York: HarperCollins, 1956.

MacNeil, Neil, and Richard A. Baker. *The American Senate: An Insider's History*. New York: Oxford University Press, 2013.

Marriott, J. A. R. *Second Chambers: An Inductive Study in Political Science*. Oxford: Clarendon, 1910.

Samuel, Terence. *The Upper House: A Journey Behind the Closed Doors of the U.S. Senate*. New York: Palgrave Macmillan, 2010.

WEBSITES

Congress for Kids

www.congressforkids.net

Find out more about the branches of government, the Constitution, and elections.

U.S. Senate: Art & History Exhibits

www.senate.gov/art/exhibits.htm

Look at artwork and photos to discover more about Senate history.

Note: Every effort has been made to ensure that the websites listed above are suitable for children, that they have educational value, and that they contain no inappropriate material. However, because of the nature of the Internet, it is impossible to guarantee that these sites will remain active indefinitely or that their contents will not be altered.

Published by **Creative Education** and **Creative Paperbacks** P.O. Box 227, Mankato, Minnesota 56002 Creative Education and Creative Paperbacks are imprints of **The Creative Company** www.thecreativecompany.us

Design and production by **Christine Vanderbeek** Art direction by **Rita Marshall** Printed in China

Photographs by Corbis (Bettmann, Blue Lantern Studio, CORBIS, JONATHAN ERNST/ Reuters, GraphicaArtis), Creative Commons Wikimedia (Francis Alexander, Mathew Brady/Beinecke Rare Book and Manuscript Library/ Yale University, Mathew Brady/ Library of Congress, Brady-Handy Collection/Library of Congress, John Oliver Buckley/U.S. Federal Government, Christie's, Theodore R. Davis/Harper's Weekly, Amos Doolittle/Library of Congress, George Grantham Bain Collection/ Library of Congress, Bob McNeely/ U.S. Federal Government, Albert Rosenthal/New York Public Library Digital Gallery, Peter F. Rothermel/ Library of Congress, State of California, State of Wyoming, J. C. Strauss/Library of Congress, United Press/Library of Congress, U.S. Congress/U.S. Federal Government, U.S. Department of State/U.S. Federal Government, U.S. Senate/U.S. Federal Government, A. M. Willard, William Emerson Strong Photograph Album/Digital Collections/Duke University Libraries), Getty Images (John Greim), Shutterstock (Ikeskinen, Svetlana Lukienko, J Main, VoodooDot)

Copyright © 2017 Creative Education, Creative Paperbacks International copyright reserved in all countries. No part of this book may be reproduced in any form without written permission from the publisher.

Library of Congress Cataloging-in-Publication Data McAuliffe, Bill. The U.S. Senate / Bill McAuliffe. p. cm. — (By the people) Includes bibliographical references and index. *Summary*: A historical survey of the United States Senate, from its beginnings to current issues, including its role in Congress and influential senators such as Daniel Webster and Hillary Clinton.

ISBN 978-1-60818-677-8 *(hardcover)* **ISBN** 978-1-62832-273-6 *(pbk)* **ISBN** 978-1-56660-713-1 *(eBook)* 1. United States. Congress. Senate— Juvenile literature. 2. Legislators— United States—Juvenile literature.

JK1276.M43 2016 328.73/071—dc23 2015039278

CCSS: RI.5.1, 2, 3, 8; RI. 6.1, 2, 4, 7; RH.6-8.3, 4, 5, 6, 7, 8

First Edition HC 9 8 7 6 5 4 3 2 1 **First Edition PBK** 9 8 7 6 5 4 3 2 1

Pictured on cover: Hiram Revels